IDEAS
TO GO

BETTER

BEHAVIOUR

Ages 8-10

Activities and ideas to develop better behaviour
across the National Curriculum

Dr Helen McGrath

BERRY HILL
D0491866

A & C Black • London

CONTENTS

Introduction ... 3

How to Use this Book ... 4

Teachers' File ... 5
About behaviour management ... 6
Classroom organisation ... 7
ICT tips ... 9
Assessment ... 10
Parental involvement ... 10

Quick Starts ... 11
Starter activities requiring little or no preparation

Circle time quick starts ... 16

Activity Bank ... 17
27 photocopiable activities

Conflict and anger management
Fights: proceed with CAUTION! ... 18
Sorting it out ... 19
Which one? ... 20
Dealing with anger ... 21
Draw these angry phrases ... 22
Angry language ... 23

Developing relationships through work and play
Find your match ... 24
Conversation starters ... 25

Being accepted ... 26
Friendly fairy cakes ... 27
Meeting badges ... 28
Rules for our classroom discussions ... 29
Positive or negative thinker? ... 30
Encouragement balloons ... 31
Is this telling tales? ... 32
Did they really *mean* to do it? ... 33

Developing confidence
Independence! ... 34
Key to success ... 35
What am I good at? ... 36

Developing good relationships
What is cooperation? ... 37
Community cooperation ... 38
Teacher/class feedback ... 39
Thank you for your support! ... 40
Certificate for thoughtfulness ... 40
Classroom contract ... 41
Reward time ... 42
Group work ... 43

Challenges ... 44
Task cards that offer creative challenges

Good and bad friends ... 45
Surprise boxes ... 45
Time capsule ... 46
Angry feelings mobile ... 46
Paper plate feedback ... 47
'Getting to know us' kit ... 47
Friendly trivia quiz ... 48
Teasing rubbish ... 48

INTRODUCTION

Effective behaviour management has three elements – prevention, 'on-the-spot' management and ongoing behavioural support. Most effort should be put into prevention, to make it less likely that pupils will choose to misbehave. Providing a positive and supportive classroom environment, where pupils are taught specific social and personal skills, will help to ensure that pupils feel safe and accepted at school. This book provides teachers with ideas, activities and strategies to help pupils develop the skills to positively manage their own behaviour and also gives suggestions for dealing with challenging behaviour. The activities can be used to complement classroom work, or as a strategic resource for a particular situation.

ABOUT THIS BOOK

TEACHERS' FILE

The teachers' file offers advice on how to make make the most of this book. It contains ideas for classroom organisation as well as background notes, ICT tips, assessment ideas and suggestions for parental involvement.

QUICK STARTS

This section offers activities, games and ideas that will help teachers to improve pupils' abilities to manage their own behaviour. These activities can be used at any time, with little or no preparation, in any order, and incorporated into the classroom curriculum. Also included in this section is a 'Circle time quick starts' page which gives ideas and simple rules for establishing the use of circle time as part of the classroom routine.

ACTIVITY BANK

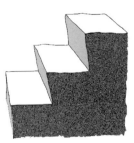

Photocopiable activities

The activity bank contains 27 photocopiable activities covering aspects of behaviour management related to the Knowledge, Skills and Understanding outlined in the guidelines for PSHE and Citizenship at Key Stages 1 and 2 (see QCA initial guidance, published in April 2000). The activities can be used in any order and may be modified and adapted to suit individual pupils, classes or schools. The activity sheets will be most effective when used to follow up a group or whole-class discussion.

CHALLENGES

These photocopiable task cards offer creative challenges to individual pupils, pairs or groups. They can be given at any time and in any sequence. In order to complete these tasks pupils need to be able to follow the instructions, independent of the teacher.

HOW TO USE THIS BOOK

QUICK STARTS

Quick starts contains a variety of short activities that can be used at any time during the day. They offer suggestions for relationship games, building positive routines, team cooperation, and recognising and rewarding good behaviour. These activities are intended to encourage the children to reflect on individual and general class behaviour.

Example

Identifying feelings (page 13) is ideal for encouraging pupils to think about different ways they can express their emotions.

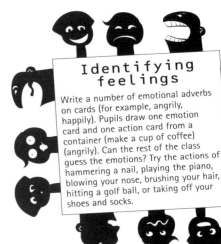

Identifying feelings

Write a number of emotional adverbs on cards (for example, angrily, happily). Pupils draw one emotion card and one action card from a container (make a cup of coffee) (angrily). Can the rest of the class guess the emotions? Try the actions of hammering a nail, playing the piano, blowing your nose, brushing your hair, hitting a golf ball, or taking off your shoes and socks.

ACTIVITY BANK

These photocopiable activities can be used by individuals, groups or the whole class. They could provide the focus for a whole lesson and are important in promoting valuable discussion. The activities in themselves will not achieve the objectives, but they will make the children start to think about their behaviour and its effect on others. Some of the activities will touch on personal issues and this should be taken into consideration when introducing activities and discussing outcomes.

Example

Encouragement balloons (page 31) is ideal for helping pupils to support and encourage others to make improvements in their behaviour and work.

BLM 13 NAME: Stewart Allen

Encouragement Balloons

In the speech balloons, write encouraging messages for someone who is trying to improve their behaviour or do better work. Some ideas: You can do it!; Great work!

Colour the balloons in different colours and cut them out. Pin your balloons to the classroom's 'Encouragement Board'. When you wish to encourage someone, choose a message and place it on their desk.

Come on, I know you can do it.

Try your hardest.

Keep trying.

Try and think harder.

Your work will improve if you try

Join up your letters and and you have better handwriting

CHALLENGES

These activities are perfect for use in independent learning sessions where the focus is social interaction. They provide more practical activities for reinforcing behaviour management strategies previously covered in this book.

Example

Paper plate feedback (page 47) allows children and adults to indicate how they are feeling about classroom situations.

TASK CARD 5 ## Paper plate feedback

What you need:
• two plain paper plates for each person
• lollipop sticks
• glue
• felt-tip pens

What to do:
1. On one side of a paper plate draw a happy face and on the other side an unhappy face.
2. Glue a lollipop stick to the bottom to use as a handle.
3. On another paper plate, draw an angry face on one side and a worried face on the other side.
4. Now you have four feeling messages to give to your teacher.
5. When your teacher asks 'Did you like that activity?', hold up the face which describes how you felt about it.
6. When your teacher asks 'How do you feel about this idea?', hold up the face which describes how you feel about it.
7. Make one set for your teacher which they can use to show how they feel about your behaviour or work.

TEACHERS' FILE

ABOUT BEHAVIOUR MANAGEMENT

Why do pupils misbehave?

- They feel as though they don't belong and so act out by misbehaving or getting into fights and arguments.
- They do not feel any sense of personal success at school.
- They do not have the personal skills to manage their behaviour and feelings.
- They feel disempowered because of negative feedback, either from peers or teachers, and express their anger through aggression or rule breaking.

There are also many reasons why groups of pupils misbehave, such as:

- What they are learning appears irrelevant, uninteresting or is taught in an unengaging fashion.
- There is a competitive and negative classroom climate.
- Pupils do not know each other well and have not developed positive relationships with each other.
- Expectations about how they should behave have not been made clear.
- Pupils do not have opportunities to learn to behave responsibly through decision making or undertaking important tasks.

'On-the-spot' management

It is important to deal with negative behaviour quickly and effectively. Apply appropriate and graduated consequences and where possible let the punishment 'fit the crime'.

Behavioural support

Some pupils find it more difficult than others to change their behaviour. For these pupils you may need to provide ongoing support, such as:

- An individual support plan which identifies what behavioural support will be offered, how and by whom.
- Peers to support them in changing their behaviour, e.g. a circle of friends.
- An individual behaviour contract between pupil and teacher with follow up rewards.
- Re-teaching of some specific skills in small groups.

Prevention

Build relationships and trust   Relationship building helps to develop a positive and supportive classroom climate. Use activities and games to help pupils get to know and like each other.

Create a good relationship between yourself and your pupils   Start with an expression of warmth and encouragement, focusing on their strengths rather than their weaknesses. Find something special about each pupil which you can talk to them about. Showing an interest in pupils will help to create a good working relationship.

Teach social skills   Becoming more socially skilful enhances pupils' relationships with each other and creates a positive culture. You can teach pupils specific social skills, such as sharing, cooperating, resolving conflict, being positive, showing empathy, and maintaining friendships.

Teach personal skills   You can also teach pupils personal skills which contribute to cooperation and self-discipline, such as anger management, understanding and handling feelings, being independent, and setting and achieving goals.

Establish a strong anti-bullying program   Establish within the school that all forms of bullying are unacceptable. This may take a while but it is essential for creating the kind of safe, supportive and accepting environment which underpins good behaviour management.

Establish reward programs for appropriate behaviour   Use strategies, games and activities which encourage good behaviour, such as finishing work, paying attention, not disrupting others and cooperating in groups. Set up rewards systems which are not expensive, do not attract envy from classmates, and are relevant to what is happening in the classroom (where possible).

Build classroom relationships

Set aside some time every day in the first few weeks of term to start building a positive, supportive classroom environment. Use activities which help pupils get to know more about each other, using random groupings to enable each pupil to work at some point with every other classmate. Have pupils play educational games where they can have fun together and develop positive relationships so they feel safe to speak openly to each other. Give pupils many opportunities to make class decisions, give you feedback, and to negotiate.

Directly teach social skills, such as sharing and taking turns, listening well, being positive, negotiation, conflict management and respectful disagreeing. Use the four-step method when teaching social skills:

- discuss the skill
- outline the steps of how to gain the skill
- have pupils practise the skill using drama
- have pupils use the skill in a real activity, and give feedback.

Try to use cooperative learning at least once a day. It will not only improve the quality of learning for your pupils, but will also allow them opportunities to practise social skills and build relationships with each other.

Rights, responsibilities, relationships

Effective discipline is based on rights, responsibilities and relationships.
Pupils have the right to:

- the freedom to be themselves.
- the protection of both themselves and the things they own.
- the ability to concentrate on and enjoy their work without serious interruption.
- classroom surroundings which allow them to learn.
- a healthy and safe environment.

When a pupil violates one of these rights, you can ask 'Is what you're doing right or wrong?' Then extend this into a discussion about how their negative behaviour has affected the other pupils.

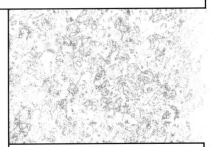

Catch 'em being good

Establish effective reward systems which encourage good behaviour. Set up ways of giving whole class rewards when, as a group, they behave well. When necessary, negotiate individual contracts with specific pupils who are having more trouble than the others getting it right. With individual pupils you can either use individual rewards, or group rewards which they can earn and donate to the whole class (for example, group games).

Use buddy systems

Cross-age buddy systems are an integral part of good behaviour management. For the older buddy, there are gains in maturity, empathic thinking, responsibility and social skills. Older pupils are less likely to give younger pupils a hard time when there are buddy systems in place, and more likely to act in a mature manner around their buddies. For the younger buddy there is the obvious benefit of a greater sense of safety, as well as feeling connected to an older pupil. The younger buddy also has the opportunity to see good social skills modelled.

Problem-solving mat

Teach the skills of conflict management. Make a 'Problem-solving mat' where pupils can be sent, or chose to go to sort out their conflict management issues. Tell pupils if they can't resolve things, you will mediate. Individual pupils could also use this mat as a place for 'time out' or for calming down.

Circle time

It is important to set aside some time each week where issues such as behaviour can be addressed as a whole class. It is an ideal time to allow pupils to discuss and explore their thoughts and feelings on a wide range of issues and events. Three simple rules should be established so that all pupils know:

- they must wait their turn before talking
- they must listen carefully to others
- they should show their interest by looking at the speaker.

A chance to shine

Give pupils the opportunity to take on responsible jobs at school, which will allow them to show others that they can organise, cooperate, lead and act confidently and gives them a sense of belonging. Use a range of teaching strategies that reflect different styles of learning, i.e. visual, auditory or kinaesthetic. Keep a record of your observations of pupils' relative strengths. On page 36 you will find an activity called 'What am I good at?' for pupils to complete.

Classroom contracts

The most useful classroom contract is one that is negotiated between teacher and pupils and is relevant to their particular classroom climate. It should be introduced within the first week of term so that pupils are quickly aware of the behaviour expectations set. Page 41 features a classroom contract that will establish a commitment to positive behaviour.

Effective teaching

Effective teachers have fewer problems with behaviour management. Use engaging teaching strategies which are active and give pupils opportunities to socialise with each other in structured ways. Generate high curiosity by using many activities based around critical and creative thinking. Have fun with your pupils and express encouragement towards them. Be fair and consistent in the way you apply rules and deal with disputes, treating each individual pupil with respect. Share parts of yourself with your pupils and make what you teach relevant to pupils' lives.

Independence and cooperation

Explain to pupils that you expect them to think for themselves ('be their own boss'), and be helpful and work with you and other pupils in the classroom.

Teach cooperation and respect through discussion, and using the activities in this book. Try to use these terms when talking to pupils about their behaviour.

Refer to these behaviour styles when reprimanding pupils. For example, 'We try to be helpful in our classroom. How can you be more helpful?'; or by giving them positive feedback, 'Thank you for working well with the others. It made our class much better.'

Partner computer games

Working on the computer is a useful context for teaching thoughtfulness and good manners. Arrange for pairs of pupils to play computer games together when feasible. Before they start, ask them to repeat for you the social skills required for working with partners. These are social skills such as:

- sharing and taking turns
- playing fairly and by the rules
- being a good winner and being a good loser
- paying attention to the game rather than being distracted
- having your go reasonably quickly rather than stalling.

Computer time as a reward

Make computer time with a friend of their choice a reward for different behaviours, such as completion of work, improved behaviour for periods of time, or no hassles at playtime or lunchtime. Put a limit on the amount of time which can be earned as reward time, or make the amount of time earned reflect the degree of behavioural improvement. Alternatively have a reward menu on the computer so that individual pupils can browse the menu and select which reward they would like to earn. They can then set up their behaviour contract with the teacher using their ICT skills. Here are some ideas for rewards:

- helping out in a younger class for a session
- listening to music with headphones
- selecting a game to play with a group
- choosing an art and craft activity such as model making.

Email feedback

Set up contact between a pupil and another significant adult in the school, whereby the pupil emails the adult (possibly another teacher or the deputy headteacher) when they have had periods of good behaviour or achieved goals. This tactic can also be used with parents if there is email at home.

Computer tutors

Even at an early age some pupils show an ability to quickly learn computer skills, especially if they have access to a computer at home. Put together a 'Computer Advisory Committee' of pupils who have knowledge and skills in specific areas of technology. This committee can be called on to teach others in the class a specific skill, assist the teacher, or be 'loaned' to another class as advisers. Similarly establish a 'Graphics Committee' of pupils who can easily produce computer graphics for posters, contracts, or certificates.

ASSESSMENT

Behaviour issues can be assessed by observing a pupil or group of pupils over time. Keeping a set of observations or record of events will enable you to compile an overall picture of behaviour patterns.

Observations

During observations of pupils ask yourself a number of questions that will provide useful information.

- What happens before he/she misbehaves?
- Does the behaviour occur in a particular place?
- Is there a certain pupil usually present?
- What are the specific behaviours that concern you?
- What positive reaction is the misbehaviour attracting, if any?

Encourage pupils to assess their own behaviour. This could involve a regular meeting between pupil and teacher, keeping a daily comment book or using some of the self evaluating worksheets in the activity bank.

PARENTAL INVOLVEMENT

It is important that pupil, teacher and parents work together when addressing behavioural issues. Parents need to be supportive of the school's approach to dealing with these problems. Good communication within this triangle is vital. Don't forget parents also need to hear about the improvements and achievements their child makes.

Encouraging news

Pupils get a real buzz when you tell their parents good things about them. Tell parents about improvements in behaviour or attitude using suggestions in the activity bank. Be as specific as possible (for example, 'Emma has now developed a good relationship with two other girls in the class'). Make sure that certificates earned by pupils go home to their parents, and compile a list of certificates earned by each pupil.

The 'back of the door trick'

Send home a sheet with information about a skill you are working on, and ask parents to put a copy of the sheet somewhere where their child will see it. The back of the toilet door is a good place or under a fridge magnet.

Classroom photographic records

Take photographs of the life of the classroom and have pupils write descriptions. Let pupils take them home to show their parents. Make these available for parent-teacher interviews.

QUICK STARTS

Collections

Nominate two pupils to be curators who will establish collections (objects, ornaments, documents, tickets, photographs, brochures) around a current class theme. Curators suggest relevant items, invite fellow pupils to contribute, ensure safe acceptance and return of property, design rules to make sure that items are well cared for, organise the display and return items at the end of the time period. This develops responsibility and cooperation.

Secret signals

Establish private signals with pupils as prompts, for example a winding-up gesture to communicate to someone who is 'winding up' or getting overexcited that they need to settle down. Use the 'hang loose' gesture with angry or upset pupils. Make a fist, put up the thumb and the little finger and move your hand in a rocking motion. Try a 'mouth zip' for talkative pupils.

Mexican waves

Discuss how most people don't like raised voices. Explain that you will ask one group to start a silent Mexican wave when you want the class to stop work, quieten down and listen to you. As soon as each pupil sees the Mexican wave, they should stop talking and join in. The ripple effect will have the class silent very quickly. Remind pupils to be silent and not silly in the way they do this.

Teachers are people too!

Discuss with pupils your own behaviours which you are prepared to try to improve, and will take responsibility for if you don't. This models the process of self-control and goal setting for pupils. For example you could have a consequence of no homework for the class if you raise your voice more than twice a day, or if you forget to do something which you agreed to do.

Conversation opportunities

Give pupils an opportunity to practise the social skills of good listening and being interesting. Compile a list of suitable topics for pupils to talk about. Allocate pupils into groups of three for a fifteen minute session. Before each conversation session, remind pupils of the skills to be used. Pupils can use a reflection book to record how well they think they used 'good listening' and 'being interesting' skills.

Identifying feelings

Write a number of emotional adverbs on cards (for example, angrily, happily). Pupils draw one emotion card and one action card from a container, e.g. make a cup of coffee, angrily. Can the rest of the class guess the emotions? Try the actions of hammering a nail, playing the piano, blowing your nose, brushing your hair, hitting a golf ball, or taking off your shoes and socks.

Playground raffles

Use raffle tickets to improve playground behaviour. Playground duty teachers give out a raffle ticket each time they observe pupils behaving well in the playground - for example, cooperating, supporting, playing well, negotiating or including others. Ask pupils to write their names on the back of the tickets and post them into a box. At the end of the week, tickets are drawn and prizes awarded such as listening to music at lunchtime.

Class goals

One of the best ways to teach goal setting is to set a class goal and then show them step by step how to do it. Some possibilities are sponsoring a World Vision child, producing a class magazine, making a class vegetable garden, or setting up and running a schoolwide tournament - for example, Uno, Scrabble, or table tennis.

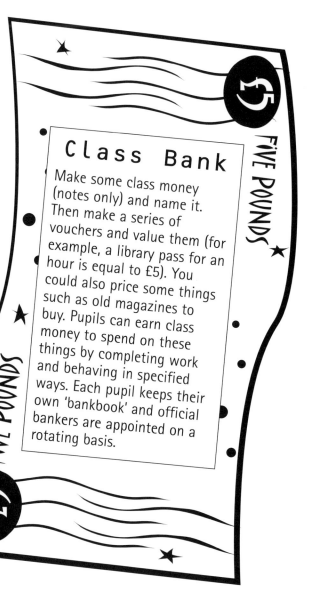

Class Bank

Make some class money (notes only) and name it. Then make a series of vouchers and value them (for example, a library pass for an hour is equal to £5). You could also price some things such as old magazines to buy. Pupils can earn class money to spend on these things by completing work and behaving in specified ways. Each pupil keeps their own 'bankbook' and official bankers are appointed on a rotating basis.

Silent speedball

Have pupils stand next to their seats, with one pupil holding a ball. The ball must be thrown within three seconds to another pupil silently, accurately and with good eye contact. This pupil in turn must immediately throw it to another, still without speaking, but with good eye contact and an accurate throw. Pupils are 'out' if they break a rule, throw poorly or fail to catch it. This focuses on self-control and good winning and losing.

Choosing groups

Let pupils know that groups will mostly be randomly put together so that all pupils get a chance to work with each other. Sometimes you can let them choose which groups they want to be in but add this proviso—'I will check in one minute. If at that time there is anyone who hasn't been invited into a group, we will disband and I will randomly group you'.

Lights off!

Turn the lights off when the whole class is being noisy and disruptive. The amount of time the lights are turned off is how long the class loses from their leisure activities, such as lunchtime or free time. (You may need to put the lights on first when you suspect that the class is getting a bit chaotic, so that you can then turn them off.)

Warning cards

Make a series of warning cards to use with individual pupils who are off-task or misbehaving—'This is a first and last warning to you that your behaviour is currently unacceptable. Please make a better choice.'; 'You are not getting on with your work. Please find a way to correct this.'; or 'Your behaviour is disruptive to others. If this doesn't stop I will ask you to move.'

Cut-throat

Have pupils play in two teams of three for five rounds. Each player in turn throws a dice, adding the amount shown on the dice to their individual score. Players are disqualified if they throw a six. If they go out their score is not included for their team. The aim is to be the team with the highest score. Pupils must avoid nasty comments and anger towards others.

Circle of friends

Establish a 'circle of friends', that is three caring and kind-natured pupils who can offer support and assist a pupil with self-control. The circle should offer this support on an ongoing basis in a non-bossy way (for example by putting a hand on his/her arm when he/she is getting upset). They can also help him/her stay on-task. A circle of friends can also help to introduce an isolated pupil into games and activities.

Because you deserve it!

Every now and then, just because things are going well and pupils are working well, stop in the middle of the day and say 'We're going to have a game (or ten minutes free time) because you have all been working so hard (or getting along so well) that you really deserve it.'

 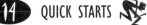

Re-energising centre

Have a section of your classroom furnished with cushions, beanbags and magazines where pupils can go when they are feeling tired, not able to work and/or likely to misbehave. Once a week they can check themselves into this re-energising centre with permission. They must use it by themselves and cannot stay for any longer than fifteen minutes. They must record when they arrive and leave the centre.

Games rewards

Set aside a number of good group games that pupils can only play if they successfully practise, as a class, a social skill a certain number of times. Skills might include completing work on time, getting on well together, and having no teasing or upsetting episodes. Use a chart with a certain number of circles (see page 42), which can be coloured in each time the behaviour occurs.

Up close and personal

When you need to reprimand a pupil or give a direct instruction, don't call out to them from across the room. Reprimands should always be given privately, not publicly, to avoid resentment and alienation. You should go over to the pupil, get down to around their height so you can make firm eye contact, stand reasonably close to them and then deliver your message.

Time out

Remove a pupil from socialising and working with others on enjoyable tasks when necessary. Make sure that this period is boring and allows no communication with other pupils. Don't make it vague and unlimited, such as 'you can return when you have improved your attitude'. Instead, be specific about exactly how long it is for and what rule they have broken (for example 'You have broken the rule about not disrupting others. Please take Time Out for five minutes.').

Hassle-free jars

Have a hassle-free jar for playground rewards. Draw smiley faces on 40 ping-pong balls. Teachers on playground duty place a ping-pong ball into a jar whenever they have had a 'hassle-free' playtime; that is, no pupils behaved in ways which required teachers to intervene. When the lid of the jar won't fit on, the whole school gets extra play time.

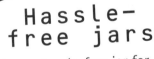

CIRCLE TIME QUICK STARTS

Circle time has become an important part of the Key Stage 1 timetable. It is flexible enough to be used in most subject areas and can naturally link areas of the curriculum. It is particularly appropriate for discussions raised within the PSHE and Citizenship Framework.

Say hello

It is important that a class of children are given opportunities to get to know each other. Sitting in a circle ensures everybody can see all the pupils in their class. A simple beginning to circle time is to pass around a 'Hello' accompanied by a handshake. Repeat the exercise adding more information each time. For example, 'Hello, my name is Andrew.' Next time you might say, 'Hello, my name is Andrew and I have got a pet dog called Bobby.'

Circle time etiquette

Three simple rules should be followed when carrying out a circle time session:
• Only talk when it is your turn.
• Listen carefully to the child who is talking.
• Look towards the child that is talking.

To help the children learn these rules, choose a circle time object such as a teddy bear. Tell the children they can only talk when they have the teddy bear sitting on their lap. This will encourage them to focus on the pupil with the chosen object. The object used at circle time can be changed for each session.

Discussing feelings

Circle time is a useful tool for dealing with current issues or events that are upsetting children in the class. Place key words such as sad, worried, unhappy or lonely in the middle of the circle and ask children to discuss when or what makes them feel like this. This can be particularly good for following events that have happened in the playground, for example a child being excluded by their group of friends. When discussions of this nature are taking place it is important to use the 'no names' rule. The 'no names' rule means that pupils are not allowed to name other children in the school who have caused these feelings.

Magic stone

Circle time sessions can be used to encourage children's creativity and imagination. Give them an interesting object like a large smooth pebble and tell them it is magical. Ask a child to rub the magic stone and describe what they imagine would happen next!

Character hats

Put a selection of hats in the middle of the circle and give the pupils a situation. The children can chose the character they wish to play, and may use a hat or any other props they feel are in role. The situation can then be acted out. You can extend this activity by asking for pupils who feel they can act out the same characters in a different way.

ACTIVITY BANK

Fights: proceed with CAUTION!

Cool off.

Accept that you both have a problem. Decide that it can be fixed.

Understand their way of seeing it. Listen to them and don't interrupt.

Talk about your concerns. Use a calm voice and start with 'I'.

Identify possible solutions to the problem.

Open up to the idea of giving way on some things to get other things.

Negotiate a way for both of you to get as much of what you want as possible.

Design your own 'CAUTION' sign below.

Teaches conflict management skills.

Sorting it out

For each of the following situations, say how you would sort it out using problem-solving negotiation.

You're playing a game with your brother and he keeps moving your counter for you when you throw the dice. Sometimes he forgets it is your turn and tries to have a second go.

I would _____

_____

_____

You are helping the teacher pack up some chairs and another kid, who is also supposed to be helping, is doing hardly any work.

I would _____

_____

_____

You have free time in class to play a game. Your friend wants to play Battleship and you would prefer to play Trivial Pursuit.

I would _____

_____

_____

A group of 12 kids get together to play a game but the game only needs 10 people.

I would _____

_____

_____

Teaches conflict management skills.

????? Which one? ?????

Decide which conflict management skills are being used in these situations. Write the answer in each box.

1. Hurting others	4. Standing up for yourself
2. Avoiding the conflict	5. Apologising
3. Asking for support	6. Negotiating

A classmate always insists on going first in any activities. They don't share or wait their turn. You say to them, 'I don't like it when you don't give someone else the chance to go first. Can you share please?'	Your older sister wants to see a film you don't want to see. Your older sister says to you 'You always want to get things your way. You are so selfish. I don't even want to go if you're going.'
This is an example of:	This is an example of:
You are playing by yourself kicking a ball when someone else kicks the ball away from you. You ask them to stop but they keep doing it. You ask the teacher on playground duty to tell them to cut it out.	You and a classmate want to read the same book in 'Quiet Reading' time after lunch. You decide between yourselves that you can take turns, so that every second day you will get to read this book.
This is an example of:	This is an example of:
Two of you end up doing the same classroom job. You think you have misread the rota so you say 'Sorry, I think I confused the dates. You do it today and I'll check the rota.'	You play football and one kid keeps hogging the ball. After the game, you sulk and think bad thoughts about that kid. You feel too anxious about what they would do if you said you were upset at the way they played.
This is an example of:	This is an example of:

Teaches conflict management skills.

Dealing with anger

Here are some good and bad ways to handle angry feelings. Colour the good ways blue and the bad ways yellow.

Blow my top!

Go for a run

Ride my bike

Play with the dog

Cuddle the cat or a stuffed toy

Talk to someone I trust about my angry feelings

Tell someone I am cross with what they did but not in an aggressive manner

Play some music I like

Go for a walk to calm down

Be by myself for a while

Breathe deeply till I calm down

Think calmly about who was in the right and whether any of it was my own fault

Think carefully about the best way to deal with things

Throw something

Yell and scream

Hit someone

Say nasty things to the person who upset me

Teaches anger management skills.

Draw these angry phrases

I blew my top!

I lost my cool!

I saw red!

I had steam coming out of my ears!

I gave them a piece of my mind!

I really lost it!

Teaches anger management skills.

Angry language

The language we use can influence how angry we get, whether we stay angry and how the other person responds to what we say.

Work in a small group to order these statements according to the intensity of the anger. It might be easier if you cut the boxes out to order them. Number the boxes with your final order. Compare your results with those of other groups.

I am cross because...			
I am concerned because...	I feel uncomfortable because...	I am worried because...	I feel angry because...
I feel outraged because...	I am irritated because...	I feel incensed because...	I am annoyed because...
I am upset because...	I feel disappointed because...	I feel furious because...	I feel miffed because...

Teaches anger management skills.

Find your match

Find someone in your class who:

has been to the same number of schools as you.

_____

has the same shoe size as you.

_____

has the same favourite take-away food as you.

_____

has the same cereal for breakfast as you.

_____

has two games the same as you at home.

_____

has been to the same place for a holiday as you.

_____

has the same favourite pop group as you.

_____

has the same number of brothers and sisters as you.

_____

You cannot use the same person twice.

Builds classroom relationships/getting to know others.

Conversation starters

Read the conversation starters below and decide how good they would be at helping you make friends at a new school. Rate them from one (best) to 10 (worst) and explain why you rated them this way.

☐ I was wondering if you could show me how to work this calculator.

_____

_____

☐ Want some help with that?

_____

_____

☐ Your folder looks so cool!

_____

_____

☐ Where did you get that great cap?

_____

_____

☐ Do you want some company for lunch?

_____

_____

☐ I hope it stops raining, don't you?

_____

_____

☐ I just heard a great joke! Want to hear it?

_____

_____

☐ Can you tell me where the canteen is?

_____

_____

☐ Do you understand what we have to do for homework?

_____

_____

☐ Can you help me out? I'm new here and I have no one to talk to.

_____

_____

On the back of this sheet, write your own good conversation starters.

Teaches social skills and builds classroom relationships.

Being accepted

Cut out each box. On a sheet of paper, write the two headings: 'Acceptance' and 'Rejection'. Paste the behaviours which lead people to be liked by others under the heading 'Acceptance'. Paste the behaviours which lead people to be rejected under the heading 'Rejection'.

Saying nasty things

Saying kind things

Helping others

Negotiating

Being thoughtful

Being a good winner

Being a bad winner

Being a good loser

Being a bad loser

Pointing out other people's mistakes

Cheating in games

Playing fairly in games

Refusing to go 'out' in a game

Using putdowns

Arguing with a referee

Being interesting

Being boring

Being positive

Being funny

Teaches social skills.

Friendly fairy cakes

Ingredients
- Fairy cake cases
- Cake tin
- Your favourite cake mix
- Icing ingredients
- Baking tools
- An adult to help you

Instructions
- Work in small groups. Line the cake tin with fairy cake cases.
- Prepare the cake mix under the supervision of your teacher or another adult.
- Pour the batter into the cake cases until they are about half full.
- Bake according to cooking instructions.
- Cool and ice.
- Write greetings to class members on the friendly tags below.
- Tape a greeting around the case of each cake.
- Present your friendly fairy cakes to your classmates.

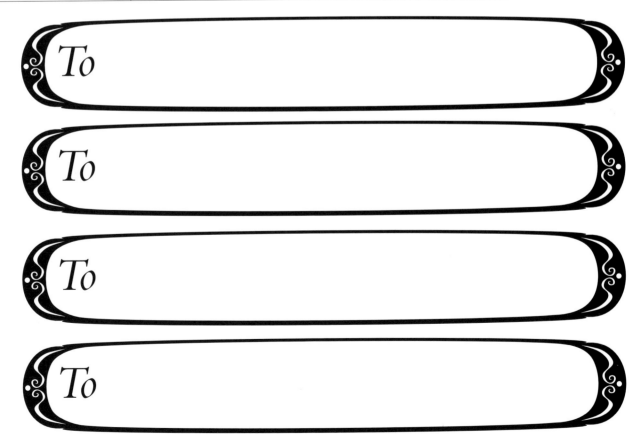

To

To

To

To

Teaches social skills and builds classroom relationships.

NAME

Meeting badges

Design your own badges for the important roles people in a meeting need to have. Glue the shapes to light cardboard, cut out and attach using safety pins.

Teaches social skills and builds classroom relationships.

Rules for our classroom discussions

- We raise our hands if we wish to speak.
  This is a good rule because

  _____

  _____

- We wait our turn until the teacher gives us permission to speak.
  This is a good rule because

  _____

  _____

- We don't speak for too long and hog the discussion.
  This is a good rule because

  _____

  _____

- This classroom is a 'no nasty comments' zone.
  This is a good rule because

  _____

  _____

- We will all try to contribute even if we feel a bit shy.
  This is a good rule because

  _____

  _____

- We respect the right of our classmates to have a different opinion.
  This is a good rule because

  _____

  _____

- We try to negotiate our decisions.
  This is a good rule because

  _____

  _____

Teaches social skills and builds classroom relationships.

Positive or negative thinker?

Take these tests to see if you are more of a positive thinker or a negative thinker.
Everyone does both, but most people think one way more than the other.

Give yourself a score for each question.

Negative thinking	I do it a lot 3 points	I do it sometimes 2 points	I rarely do it 1 point
Complain about things			
Criticise other people			
Put others down			
Compete in a conversation			
Find the bad things in my day to talk about			
Always think the worst will happen			
Find mistakes in things			

How did you score?
17–21: You are a negative thinker and need to change!
11–16: You are only a mild negative thinker but you could improve.
10 or less: You are getting the balance about right.

Positive thinking	I do it a lot 3 points	I do it sometimes 2 points	I rarely do it 1 point
Genuinely compliment people			
Talk to others about their good points and what they do well			
Find the good things about myself			
Encourage others			
Find the good things that happen in my day to talk about			
Assume the best will happen			
Ignore mistakes in things and not make a big deal of them			

How did you score?
14–21: You are a positive thinker!
9–13: You are reasonably positive but you could improve.
8 or less: You need to make a plan to become more of a positive thinker.

Teaches social and personal skills.

Encouragement balloons

In the speech balloons, write encouraging messages for someone who is trying to improve their behaviour or do better work. Some ideas: You can do it!; Great work!

Colour the balloons in different colours and cut them out. Pin your balloons to the classroom's 'Encouragement Board'. When you wish to encourage someone, choose a message and place it on their desk.

Reinforces classroom values and teaches social skills.

Is this telling tales?

- **Telling tales** is trying to get someone into trouble and not trying to solve the problem yourself.
- **Asking for support** is asking a teacher to help you solve a serious problem that you haven't been able to solve by yourself.
- **Acting responsibly** is letting a teacher or other adult know when something damaging or dangerous is happening to you or someone else in your class.

Story one

You notice that three boys from your class are teasing another classmate. They call him names, take his things and have started to trip him up every time they see him. You decide to let your teacher know what is going on.

Which of the three are you using?

_____

Story two

Three older pupils keep taking the ball you and your friends play with at lunchtime. You and your friends keep asking them to stop but they just make fun of you. You finally decide to talk to the teacher on playground duty about it.

Which of the three are you using?

_____

_____

Story three

You are playing with three other kids from your class when you decide you don't want to play any more. One of the other kids yells in anger, 'You can't play in our games again!' You go to the teacher on duty and say, 'They say if I don't play now I can't ever play with them again.'

Which of the three are you using?

_____

_____

Teaches personal skills.

Did they really *mean* to do it?

How good are you at knowing whether someone really meant to hurt you or if it was an accident?

When someone has deliberately hurt you and is trying to be mean you know because:

This is what they say: _____

_____

This is how they say it: _____

_____

This is what their face looks like:

When someone hurt you by accident and they were not trying to be mean, you know because:

This is what they say: _____

_____

This is how they say it: _____

_____

This is what their face looks like:

Teaches the personal skill of intention detection.

Independence!

List all the ways in which you can act independently and be your own boss.

When I don't know how to do something in my work, and I need help but the teacher is busy with another pupil, I can act independently by

_____

_____

_____

When I am being annoyed by someone else in the class who is trying to make me laugh, I can act independently by

_____

_____

_____

When I can't find my pencils in my desk and the teacher is talking to someone else, I can act independently by

_____

_____

_____

When I want to borrow something from someone but I feel worried that they won't lend it to me, I can act independently (instead of asking the teacher to do it for me) by

_____

_____

_____

Expects and encourages independence and cooperation.

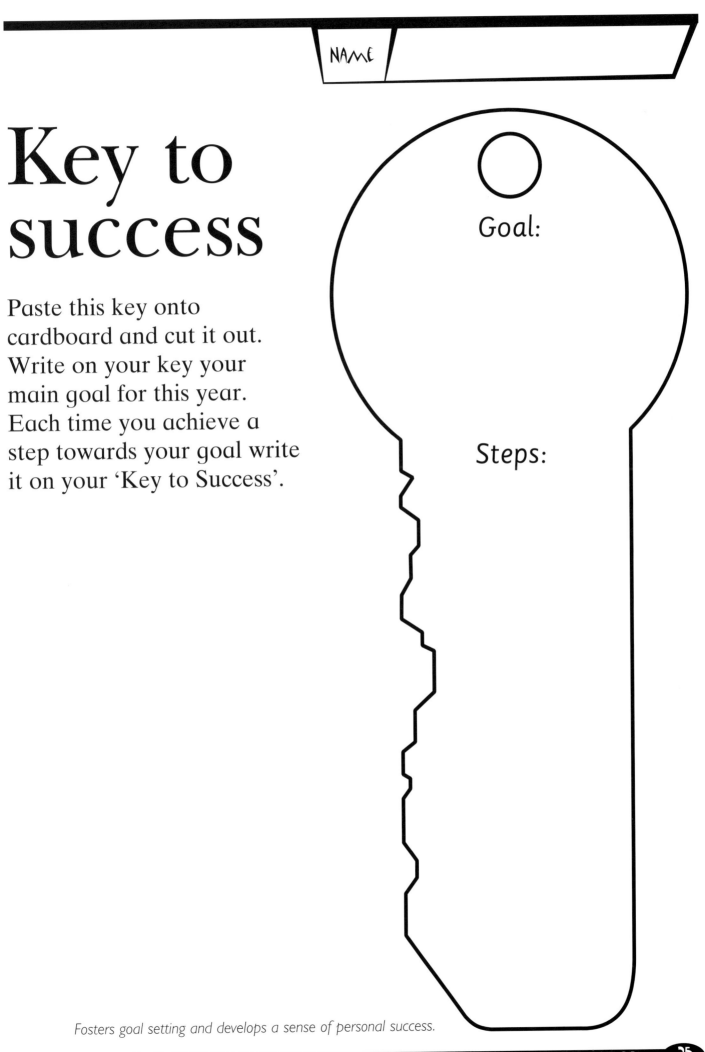

NAME

Key to success

Paste this key onto cardboard and cut it out. Write on your key your main goal for this year. Each time you achieve a step towards your goal write it on your 'Key to Success'.

Goal:

Steps:

Fosters goal setting and develops a sense of personal success.

What am I good at?

Colour in these eight different ways to be smart. Glue them onto cardboard, and cut them out. Put these ways of being smart in a pile, with the thing you are best at on top. Put the other seven ways in order underneath. (Remember, you only need to be good at MOST of the things inside a drawing to choose it as one of the ways you are smart.)

Next, ask your teacher or a parent to sort them from one to eight to show what they think you are best at.

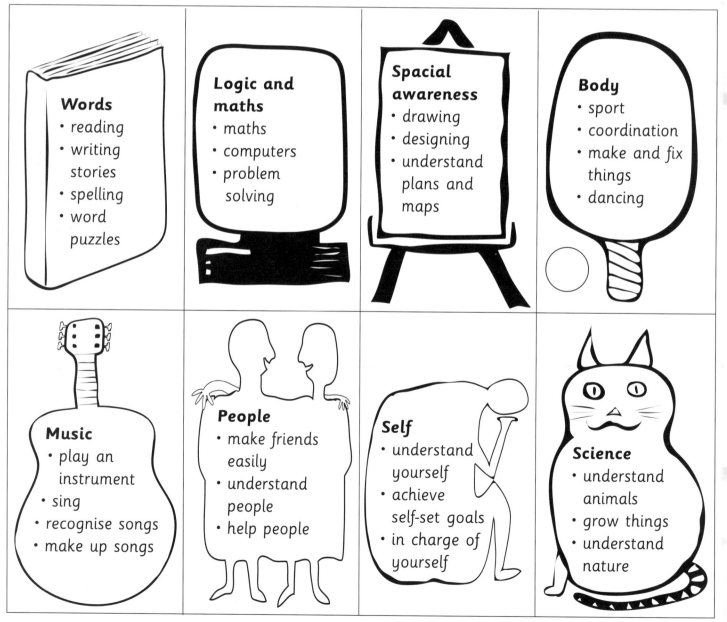

Words
• reading
• writing
  stories
• spelling
• word
  puzzles

Logic and maths
• maths
• computers
• problem
  solving

Spacial awareness
• drawing
• designing
• understand
  plans and
  maps

Body
• sport
• coordination
• make and fix
  things
• dancing

Music
• play an
  instrument
• sing
• recognise songs
• make up songs

People
• make friends
  easily
• understand
  people
• help people

Self
• understand
  yourself
• achieve
  self-set goals
• in charge of
  yourself

Science
• understand
  animals
• grow things
• understand
  nature

Encourages children to recognise their strengths.

What is cooperation?

Give two examples of cooperation which occur:

• in your home

1. _____

2. _____

• between pupils in this class

1. _____

2. _____

• between teachers at your school

1. _____

2. _____

Describe three ways better cooperation by class members would help your classroom to be a more enjoyable place.

1. _____
_____

2. _____
_____

3. _____
_____

Expects and encourages independence and cooperation.

Community cooperation

Fill in the table below with examples of cooperation in our community.

Where people cooperate	How they cooperate	Why they cooperate	Result if they didn't cooperate
picnic area	put rubbish in bin	everyone can enjoy a clean space	dirty picnic area; would be unhealthy and ugly

List two situations where total chaos or danger would occur if people in our community didn't cooperate.

_____

_____

Design a poster on the back of this sheet which encourages people to cooperate more when driving.

Expects and encourages independence and cooperation.

Teacher/class feedback

How many pupils in this class seem to like each other?

- All of them
- Most of them
- Some of them
- None of them

How many pupils in this class act in a friendly and caring way to each other?

- All of them
- Most of them
- Some of them
- None of them

How many pupils in this class are mean to each other?

- Most of them
- Some of them
- None of them

How many pupils in this class behave badly and stop others from working?

- None of them
- Some of them
- Many of them

Which of these descriptions best fits our class? Pick just one.

- It is a very friendly classroom where you feel safe.
- It is quite a friendly classroom but some people can be mean to you.
- It is not a friendly classroom and sometimes I feel scared about how the other kids will behave.

Encourages pupil feedback.

Thank you for your support!

This support certificate has been awarded to

_____

for the support which was given to

_____

in the form of

_____

_____

_____

_____   _____

Teacher's signature   Date

Certificate for thoughtfulness

This thoughtfulness certificate is awarded to

_____

for the thoughtfulness they showed when they

_____

_____

_____

_____   _____

Teacher's signature   Date

Develops social and moral responsbility.

Classroom contract

This is a contract between pupils in Class _____

and their teacher _____ .

It was drawn up on _____ .

We, the pupils in Class _____, agree to

_____

_____

I, _____ (teacher of Class _____) agree to give pupils

_____

_____

If the pupils fulfil their part of the contract, I will colour in one circle on a chart every time I see this being done or it is accurately reported to me. They will need _____ circles coloured in to reach their goal.

Teacher's signature: _____

Pupils' signatures: (Pupils can also sign on the back of this sheet.)

Establishes reward systems.

Reward time

One circle will be coloured in by the teacher whenever the skill or behaviour of _____

is reported or observed being used by a member of Class _____ .

We need _____ *coloured circles to earn the reward of*

_____

Establishes reward systems.

Group work

Date:

People in our group:

_____   _____   _____

_____   _____   _____

The activity we did was:

Circle your answers to the following questions.

How well did your group use the skill of _____ in today's session?

We used it really well.

We used it quite well.

We used it sometimes.

We didn't use it enough.

How well did your group work together in today's session?

We worked together well.

We worked together quite well.

We worked together well sometimes.

We didn't work together well.

Describe how this skill can help a group work together.

_____

_____

_____

In what other situations could you use this skill? _____

_____

_____

Uses cooperative learning and teaches social skills.

CHALLENGES

TASK CARD 1 — Good and bad friends

What you need:

- pen
- paper
- coloured pencils
- a partner

What to do:

1. Write a story with a partner about the worst friend in the world. (You can write a song or draw a cartoon strip instead.)

2. The story should be about how someone who is normally a good friend has a spell put on them so that they break all the rules of friendship

3. Make sure you mention these things in your story—disloyalty, selfishness, letting someone down, being too critical and being 'pig-headed'.

4. Now write a story about the best friend in the world with your partner.

5. Remember to include the following—loyalty, generosity, thoughtfulness and acceptance.

TASK CARD 2 — Surprise boxes

What you need:

- three different-sized boxes (each one smaller than the next)
- different coloured paper
- felt-tip pens
- paint
- a partner

What to do:

1. Find good sayings about friendship, kindness, support for others and cooperation, or give examples where these things happened.

2. On three pieces of paper, write a different saying or example.

3. Fold the paper so you can't see the writing.

4. Put one folded piece of paper in each box. You may wish to decorate the outside of each box.

5. Put each box inside the other so you are left with the largest box.

6. Add to a pile of other surprise boxes.

7. Select a surprise box made by someone else and read what they have written.

8. Discuss with a partner.

Time capsule

What you need:

- a partner
- souvenirs of the class
- paper
- pen
- a box
- sealing tape

What to do:

1. Working with a partner, describe your favourite memories of the class in writing.
2. Make predictions about what will happen in class during the next few months.
3. Select the souvenirs you want to include in your time capsule.
4. Make a list of the souvenirs and say why you have included them.
5. Sign and date the list.
6. Put your written memories, predictions, souvenirs and list into the box.
7. Seal the box and store it safely.
8. Open at the end of the year and share what you find.

Angry feelings mobile

TASK CARD 4

What you need:

- a coat hanger
- string
- cardboard
- scissors
- felt-tip pens

What to do:

1. List all the things which have resulted in you feeling very angry.
2. Cut out shapes to go with each of these (for example a mouth shape for someone saying unkind remarks to you).
3. Write on the front of each shape what caused your angry feelings. Be brief, and don't give too many personal details. Remember the 'no names' rule.
4. On the back of each shape, write what you could do to feel less angry about this.
5. Put a hole into the top of your shape and thread string through the hole.
6. Attach your shapes to the coat hanger.
7. Display your mobile in the classroom.

TASK CARD 5 — Paper plate feedback

What you need:

- two plain paper plates
- lollipop sticks
- glue
- felt-tip pens

What to do:

1. On one side of a paper plate draw a happy face and on the other side draw an unhappy face.
2. Glue a lollipop stick to the bottom to use as a handle.
3. On another paper plate, draw an angry face on one side and a worried face on the other side.
4. Now you have four feeling messages to give to your teacher.
5. When your teacher asks 'Did you like that activity?', hold up the face which describes how you felt about it.
6. When your teacher asks 'How do you feel about this idea?', hold up the face which describes how you feel about it.
7. Make one set for your teacher which they can use to show how they feel about your behaviour or work.

TASK CARD 6 — 'Getting to know us' kit

What you need:

- light cardboard
- paper
- pencils
- pens
- felt-tip pens, crayons
- folder or box

What to do:

1. Draw a floor plan of your classroom on cardboard showing where everyone sits.
2. List ten good things about being in this class on another piece of cardboard.
3. Decorate and illustrate your list so it becomes a poster for the noticeboard.
4. Make a three-fold brochure (using cardboard or paper) designed to encourage pupils from other classes and schools to enrol in your class.
5. Decide on two good ways that people in this class can get to know each other better.
6. Write these down and include instructions.
7. When your pieces are not on display, put them together in a folder or box titled the 'Getting to know us' kit.

Friendly trivia quiz

What you need:

- a friend
- pen
- paper
- craft materials

What to do:

1. Answer the following questions about a friend (without asking them).

   What food do they really hate?
   What song drives them nuts?
   What is their favourite song?
   Do they have a pet?
   What is their favourite colour?
   What are they frightened of?
   What job do they want to do when they leave school?
   What do they like to eat for lunch?
   Where did they go for their last holiday?
   What date is their birthday?
   What food do they most like?
   What film did they last see?
   Do they have any brothers and sisters?
   What upsets them?

2. Now check the accuracy of your knowledge with your friend. Give yourself one point for every question you were right about. The perfect score is 14. How accurate were you?

3. Create your own Friendly triva game. Design suitable packaging and write a set of instructions. Store the game in the classroom for others to play.

TASK CARD 8

Teasing rubbish

What you need:

- a partner
- cheap plastic rubbish bin (or a shoe box made to look like a rubbish bin)
- paper
- light cardboard
- felt-tip pens
- scissors

What to do:

1. Work with a partner.
2. Cut two sheets of paper into eight pieces each so you have a total of 16 pieces.
3. On eight pieces of paper write something that you have heard people **say** to others (or to you) which is teasing.
4. On the other eight pieces of paper write the things you have seen people **do** which are unkind. (Think about the expressions and gestures they use.)
5. You may draw pictures to go with each piece.
6. These 16 pieces are 'teasing rubbish'.
7. Post the 'teasing rubbish' into the teasing rubbish bin.
8. Using cardboard make a sign for the bin.
9. Anytime you see, or hear teasing, write it on paper (or draw it) and put it in the teasing rubbish bin.